Things We Do

A KIDS' GUIDE TO COMMUNITY ACTIVITY

by Rachelle Kreisman

with illustrations by Tim Haggerty

RED
CHAIR
·PRESS·

Please visit our website at **www.redchairpress.com** for more high-quality products for young readers.

Publisher's Cataloging-In-Publication Data
(Prepared by The Donohue Group, Inc.)

Kreisman, Rachelle.
   Things we do : a kids' guide to community activity / by Rachelle Kreisman ; with illustrations by Tim Haggerty. -- [First edition].

   pages : illustrations ; cm. -- (Start smart: community)

   Summary: In communities we not only find goods and services, but we also find places for fun and enjoyment to keep us happy and healthy. Includes fun facts.
   Interest age level: 006-009.
   Edition statement supplied by publisher.
   Includes index.
   Issued also as an ebook.
   ISBN: 978-1-939656-93-3 (library hardcover)
   ISBN: 978-1-939656-94-0 (paperback)

   1. Community life--Juvenile literature. 2. Parks--Juvenile literature. 3. Theaters--Juvenile literature. 4. Sports--Juvenile literature. 5. Museums--Juvenile literature. 6. Community life. 7. Parks. 8. Theaters. 9. Sports. 10. Museums. I. Haggerty, Tim. II. Title.

HM761 .K743 2015
307   2014957501

Illustration credits: p. 1, 5, 7, 13, 14, 15, 17, 19, 21, 22, 27, 28, 32: Tim Haggerty

Photo credits: Cover, p. 4, 10 (small), 14, 16, 18 (small), 25 (large), 26: iStock; p. 1, 5, 6, 7, 8, 9, 10, 11, 15, 19, 24, 25 (top), 26 (small), 27, 31: Shutterstock; p. 12, 13: Berkshire Theater Group; p. 17, 18 (large), 20, 22, 23, 29, 32: Dreamstime; p. 21: Bob Gambling Photo, Courtesy of the SoNo Switch Tower Museum; p. 32: Courtesy of the author, Rachelle Kreisman

This series first published by:
Red Chair Press LLC   PO Box 333   South Egremont, MA 01258-0333

Printed in the United States of America

042015 1P WRZF15

Table of Contents

Words in **bold type** are defined in the glossary.

Community

CHAPTER 1

Think about your neighborhood. What do you see? You may see people, pets, and homes. You may also see buildings, roads, cars, and trees. Your neighborhood is part of a **community**. A community is a place where people live, work, and play.

Some communities are busy cities. Others have fewer people and more land. What do they all have in common? They have places to meet people's needs. Those places include schools, hospitals, gas stations, and banks.

Do you like to have fun? You are not alone! Many people in a community work hard. They also like to do fun activities. Communities have places where people can go to do just that! Parks, movie theaters, and ice skating rinks are just a few of those places. Keep reading to learn more about the fun you can have in a community.

JUST JOKING!

Q: Where do cows go for fun?

A: To the *moo*-vies!

CHAPTER 2

Parks

Most communities have parks. They are outdoor spaces for the **public** to enjoy. Community parks are usually owned and operated by the city or state. The parks have trees for shade, grass, and flowers. They also have benches so people can sit and relax.

Parks often have playgrounds for kids. Play on the slide, swings, and monkey bars. You can also bring a ball or Frisbee to play catch. Walk, play tag, and run around. Going to the park is good exercise!

What else can you do at a park? Lots of things! Pack a lunch and have a picnic. Many parks have picnic tables. If not, bring a blanket and sit on the grass. Enjoy your food while you breathe the fresh air. Look up at the sky and see what cloud shapes you can find. Talk to others, read a book, or play a game. It's all up to you!

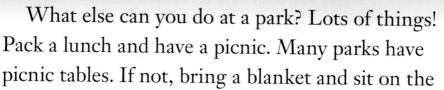

Every park is different. Some have trails to go biking or hiking. People can explore and study nature. Check out plants, flowers, and insects. Bring binoculars to be a bird-watcher.

Some parks are near the beach. Other parks are in busy cities. Dog parks are made just for people with dogs. Owners may take their dogs to play there with other dogs.

🏠 Exercise is good for *dogs and owners*.

DID YOU KNOW?

You can bike, walk, and run while helping others. How? Take part in a charity race. People who enter pay a fee. They also ask others to donate money. The money goes to help a good cause.

Some communities have **national parks**. A national park is an area of land set aside and owned by a national government. The U.S. National Park Service manages the national parks in the United States. Parks Canada manages important parks in Canada. National parks protect land and wild animals. Those animals include many **endangered species**.

National parks are for everyone to enjoy. They receive millions of visitors each year.

⌂ This tree in Sequoia Giant Forest National Park is the world's largest.

FUN FACT

What is the world's first national park? Yellowstone National Park! The land was set aside to be protected in 1872. With more than 2 million acres, the park is huge. It is larger than the states of Rhode Island and Delaware put together! Most of Yellowstone is located in Wyoming. A small area of the park is in Montana and Idaho.

GENERAL SHERMAN

CHAPTER 3

Movie Theaters

Do you like going to the movies? Lots of people do! Not all movie theaters are the same. A theater can be small and show only a few movies. Theaters can also be huge and show more than 20 movies at a time!

Some communities show movies outdoors. People can bring a blanket or chair and enjoy the movie while sitting on the grass. A few communities even have drive-in theaters. People watch the movie while sitting inside their cars.

DID YOU KNOW?

Drive-in movie theaters were popular in the 1950s and 1960s. At the time, the United States had more than 4,000 drive-ins. Today, fewer than 400 remain.

Another kind of movie theater is the IMAX. It stands for *Image MAXimum*. The images are shown on a giant curved screen. It is much larger than the screen at a regular movie theater. In addition, the IMAX movie images have more details.

Many IMAX theaters show **3-D** movies as well. Special 3-D glasses make you feel like you are part of the movie, not just watching it. Many regular movie theaters also show 3-D movies.

CHAPTER 4

Live Theater

Nothing can take the place of live theater. Theaters are places where people perform shows for an audience. The shows take place on a stage. Shows can be plays, concerts, or dance performances.

Each visit to the theater is special. Plays can be serious or funny. Concerts feature different kinds of music. Dancers perform many styles of dance. A musical is a kind of play that combines all three. It tells a story with music, song, and dance.

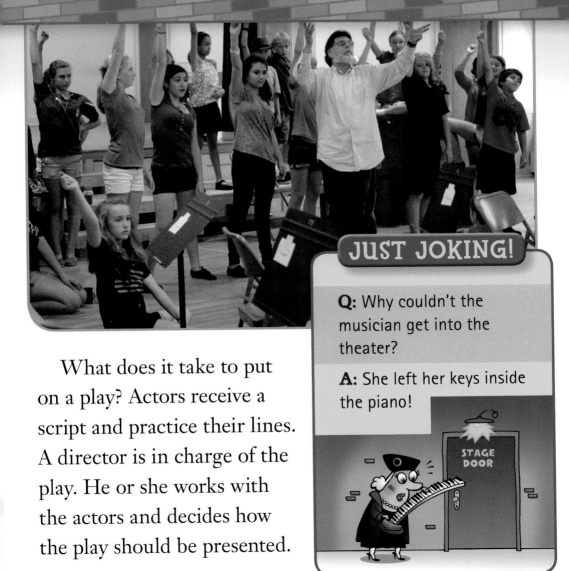

What does it take to put on a play? Actors receive a script and practice their lines. A director is in charge of the play. He or she works with the actors and decides how the play should be presented.

Designers build the scenery and create the costumes. People also make or find **props** for the show. Props are the objects used on stage, such as a telephone or books. The scenery and props used on the stage are called the **set**.

The actors spend weeks or months preparing. The final practices are called **dress rehearsals**. The actors perform in costume, without their scripts. Lighting and sound operators control the stage lights and sound effects.

On opening night, the actors go to their dressing rooms. They put on their costumes and get their makeup done. Audience members arrive and take their seats.

DID YOU KNOW?

The areas to the left and right of the stage are the wings. They are hidden from the audience's view. Actors stand in the wings until it is time to go on stage.

14

TRY THIS!

Get together with friends to put on a play. Start by choosing your favorite story and write a list of the characters. Then write a script. Decide who will play each character and practice reading your lines. Practice some more! Make costumes and have a dress rehearsal. When you are ready, put on a show for family and friends.

Each audience member receives a **program** at the door. A program is a booklet that tells about the show, the schedule, and the performers.

Now, it is time for the show! The actors do a great job. When it is over, they take a bow. Audience members clap their hands to show they liked the play.

CHAPTER 5

Sports

If you like sports, you are in luck! Communities often have places to play and watch sports. Many have soccer and baseball fields. Kids can join local teams to play. Family and friends can go to the games and cheer them on.

Are you a fan of basketball or tennis? Some communities have courts for those sports. Do you like to swim? A public pool or beach may be nearby. You may also be able to take swim lessons.

Some communities have ice-skating rinks. Kids and adults can ice skate or play ice hockey. You can rent skates or bring your own. Indoor rinks are open all year long. Outdoor rinks are open during cold weather.

Public skate times are set aside for anyone who wants to skate. Music is often played at these sessions. Rinks also offer lessons for all ages. You can learn how to skate or play ice hockey.

🏠 Hockey is great fun in winter months.

Do you like to skateboard? Some communities have skate parks. Kids can go there to practice their skateboard skills. A skate park is usually made of concrete. It has ramps, stairs, and ledges. Beginner areas have slower slopes and smaller obstacles. Advanced skaters can speed around more difficult courses.

Communities may also have roller rinks. Kids can roller skate or inline skate there. The rinks often play music so you can move to the beat.

Millions of people are sports fans. Along with playing sports, they like to watch the pros play. Some communities have college or professional teams. Athletes play at large stadiums and arenas, which can seat thousands of fans.

People can buy tickets to the games. Fans often wear team colors or **jerseys** to support their teams. Many of the games can also be seen on television so supporters can follow their community teams.

DID YOU KNOW?

The game that Americans call soccer is called football by most other countries.

CHAPTER 6

Museums

Spend time at a museum. It's a great way to learn new things! A museum is a building in which objects of interest are displayed for the public. The objects are often of art, science, or history. A collection of objects is an **exhibit**.

Most large museums are located in big cities. One of the most popular is the National Museum of Natural History. It is a science museum in Washington, D.C.

⌂ The Museum of Natural History is featured in the movie *Night at the Museum*.

FUN FACT

The National Museum of Natural History is huge. It is more than 1 million square feet! That's as big as 20 football fields. The museum's collection includes about 125 million objects.

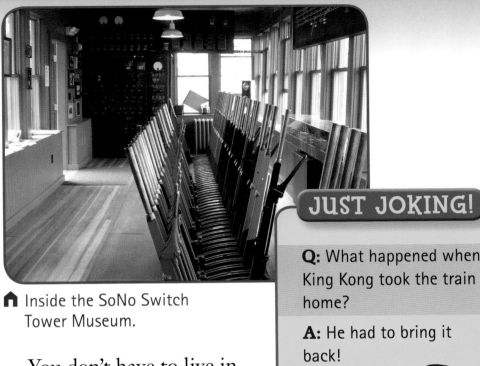

🏠 Inside the SoNo Switch Tower Museum.

You don't have to live in a big city to visit a museum. Smaller cities and towns have museums too. The museums are often smaller, but can be just as interesting.

The SoNo Switch Tower Museum in South Norwalk, Connecticut is tiny. It is located in an old railroad switch tower built in 1896. People once worked in the tower to switch trains from one track to another. Visitors climb the many steel stairs to get inside. There, they learn about train history.

Once inside a museum, take a look around. With so much to see, you may not know where to start. No problem! Museums often have maps and tours. A tour guide can lead the way and tell you about the exhibits. He or she can also answer questions.

Some museums also have audio guides. You can listen to recordings as you visit each exhibit.

🏠 Docents are guides who can tell you many interesting facts about exhibits.

🏠 The interactive news media museum, Newseum, opened in Washington D.C. in 2008.

What exhibits will you find inside a museum? It depends on where you go. From art to sports, each museum is different. You may see paintings at one museum. You may learn about dinosaurs or insects at another.

Collections can include so many things: photos, doll houses, rocks, shells, or puppets. The list goes on and on. Some communities even have children's museums. They have hands-on exhibits just for kids. Check out what museums are in or near your community!

CHAPTER 7

Community Centers

A community center is a place where people in a community gather. Centers have activities, programs, and special events. Some have fitness rooms, pools, and sports programs. They usually offer classes for all ages. Classes may include dance, arts and crafts, music, and theater.

Community centers often have programs for kids. Many centers host summer camps too.

⌂ Community centers can be a safe place to try new activities.

Some community centers are for certain age groups. Youth centers are places for kids to have fun and make new friends. Senior centers are just for **senior citizens**. Seniors often have to be age 60 and older to join. Some senior centers like to have kids visit and make friends.

Religious groups may have community centers too. The centers have activities similar to other community centers. Plus, they celebrate holidays of that religion. They also offer classes about the religion and culture.

DID YOU KNOW?

Like other community centers, senior centers often have fitness programs and classes for arts and crafts.

CHAPTER 8

So Much to Do

Communities have so many things to do. It makes life much more fun and interesting. If you feel bored, turn to your community. Take a walk in a park. Play on the playground. Visit a museum and learn something new. Go to a theater and see a play or a movie. Join a sports team or watch a game. Sign up for a class at a community center. You might even visit a senior center.

What are you waiting for? Take part in all your community has to offer! Not only will you have fun, you may also make new friends. Then you can all have fun in the community together. What do you get when you add fun and friends? A happy, healthy life!

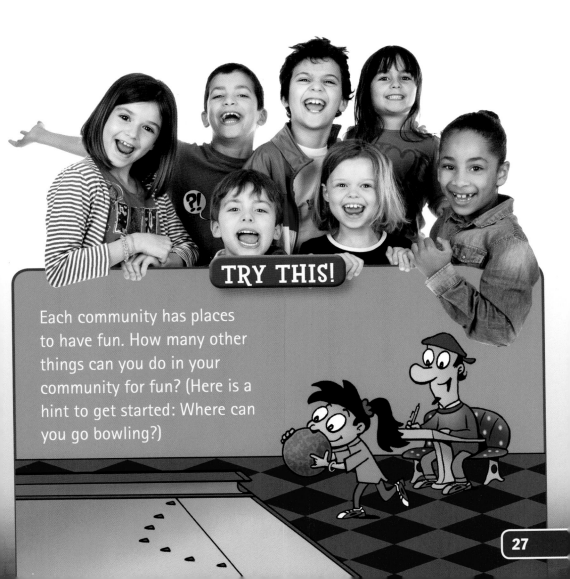

TRY THIS!

Each community has places to have fun. How many other things can you do in your community for fun? (Here is a hint to get started: Where can you go bowling?)

Glossary

community: a place where people live, work, and play

docent: a museum tour guide

dress rehearsal: the final practice of a play in full costume and makeup

endangered species: animals or plants in danger of dying out

exhibit: a collection of objects in a museum

jersey: a shirt worn as part of a sports uniform

national park: an area of land set aside and owned by a national government

program: a booklet that tells about a show, schedule, and performers

props: the objects used on stage, such as a telephone or books

public: all the people making up a community, state, or country

senior citizen: an older person, often 60 and older

set: the scenery and props used on stage during a play

3-D: something that has three-dimensions (height, width, and depth)

What Did You Learn?

See how much you learned about things to do in a community. Answer *true* or *false* for each statement below. Write your answers on a separate piece of paper.

1 Communities have places to meet people's needs.
True or false?

2 A roller rink is a place where kids can ice skate.
True or false?

3 National parks receive millions of visitors each year.
True or false?

4 Most large museums are located in small towns.
True or false?

5 An IMAX theater is a special kind of live theater.
True or false?

Answers: 1. True, 2. False (A roller rink is a place for roller skating and inline skating. An ice skating rink is a place to ice skate.), 3. True, 4. False (Most large museums are located in big cities.), 5. False (An IMAX theater is a special kind of movie theater.)

For More Information

Books

Caseley, Judith. *On the Town: A Community Adventure.* Greenwillow Books, 2002.

Hayes, Ann. *Meet the Orchestra.* Houghton Mifflin Harcourt, 1995.

Hayes, Ann. *Onstage and Backstage.* Harcourt Brace and Company, 1997.

Kaufman, Gabriel. *Sporting Events: From Baseball to Skateboarding.* Bearport Publishing Company, 2006.

Kalman, Bobbie. *What is a Community from A to Z?* Crabtree Publishing Company, 2000.

Verde, Susan. *The Museum.* Abrams Books for Young Readers, 2013.

Web Sites

CDC: BAM! Body and Mind
http://www.cdc.gov/bam/activity/cards.html

Knowitall.org
http://www.knowitall.org/kidswork/theater/history

National Parks Foundation
http://www.nationalparks.org/connect/npf-kids

National Gallery of Art
http://www.nga.gov/content/ngaweb/education/kids.html

Parks Canada for Kids
http://www.pc.gc.ca/eng/voyage-travel/xplorateurs-xplorers.aspx

Smithsonian Kids
http://www.si.edu/Kids

Note to educators and parents: Our editors have carefully reviewed these web sites to ensure they are suitable for children. Web sites change frequently, however, and we cannot guarantee that a site's future contents will continue to meet our high standards of quality and educational value. You may wish to preview these sites and closely supervise children whenever they access the Internet.

Index

About the Author

Rachelle Kreisman has been a children's writer and editor for many years. She is the author of several children's books and hundreds of *Weekly Reader* classroom magazines. When Rachelle is not writing, she enjoys going to places in her community. She likes taking walks, hiking, biking, kayaking, and doing yoga.